THE ART OF
BEATRIX POTTER

" One-and-twenty button-holes—and who should
come to sew them."

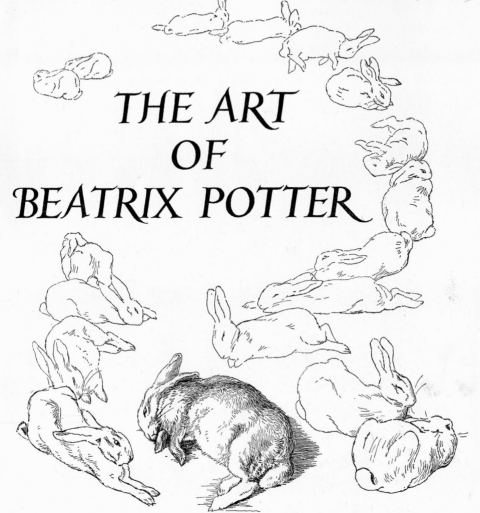

THE ART
OF
BEATRIX POTTER

With an Appreciation by Anne Carroll Moore

FREDERICK WARNE & CO. LTD. ⋅ London
FREDERICK WARNE & CO. INC. ⋅ New York

Direct reproductions of Beatrix Potter's preliminary studies and finished drawings, also examples of her original manuscript selected and arranged by L. LINDER and W. A. HERRING

Printed by THE THANET PRESS, MARGATE, KENT, ENGLAND

ACKNOWLEDGEMENTS

For the very full representation of the drawings in colour and monochrome of the late Beatrix Potter, the Publishers are greatly indebted to members of her family and friends who have made possible the reproduction of so many examples of this Artist's work, showing her great versatility.

Special thanks are due to the Executors of the late Mrs. W. Heelis (Beatrix Potter) for permission to reproduce her drawings and manuscript. Thanks are due to Capt. K. W. G. Duke, R.N., and the late Mrs. Duke for allowing access to a number of portfolios from which many of these pictures have been selected. We are indebted to the Tate Gallery for the loan of examples of her pictures from " *The Tailor of Gloucester* " now in their possession.

To the Armitt Library of Ambleside, the Publishers acknowledge the loan of examples of the Artist's drawings of Fungi.

The Publishers are also grateful to Mr. L. Linder who has loaned a number of the original drawings, and who has produced the photographs of Hill Top and Sawrey, the places associated with Beatrix Potter's life and her books.

From Mr. C. H. D. Acland of the National Trust, Messrs. E. and E. A. Heelis, Mrs. Ludbrook, Mrs. W. F. Gaddum, and Mr. W. A. Herring (who has been closely associated with the production of her books from the beginning), and others, much help and information has been received and is greatly appreciated.

CONTENTS

PART 2

BEATRIX POTTER—HER ART IN RELATION TO HER BOOKS

AN APPRECIATION

The Art of Beatrix Potter is a revelation of the hidden sources of her power as a creator of children's books of great originality and timeless value.

The living truth is here because her art is true and the selection and arrangement of the drawings permit the artist to tell her own story in line, colour and form with a reality far more convincing than the words of any writer.

It is the gift of a good book about a real person to stimulate the desire to know more. No doubt Margaret Lane's biography, *The Tale of Beatrix Potter*, with its delightful illustrations from many photographs of the artist as a child, at seventeen, in middle age and old age—and its revealing glimpses of a strong personality, may have led Mr. Leslie Linder and Mr. W. A. Herring to explore the familiar as well as the unpublished work of Beatrix Potter which lends peculiar distinction to this book. They have done so with a sure instinct for art values and an imaginative understanding of the self-development of an artist who went straight to the natural world for inspiration and to children for an appreciation of her art.

The arrangement of these direct reproductions of preliminary studies and finished drawings is by groups indicative of Beatrix Potter's strongest interests during the years she was growing up and in the period preceding the publication of her books. It is a singularly happy arrangement for it focuses attention on the artist's own approach to her work and the infinite pains she took to achieve such mastery of subject as may be found under the group headings of Houses, and Village Scenes, Interiors, Microscopic Work, Fungi, etc., of Part 1.

THE ART OF BEATRIX POTTER

Although Beatrix Potter had been drawing and painting from early childhood, her first efforts were in copying pictures of birds, butterflies and animals from books with colour plates of natural history. With her discovery of the natural world during northern holidays came the desire to give expression to what she saw so clearly in flower, animal and landscape. It was then that learning how to draw became important to her and her signature takes on significance. The flower drawing on page 32 signed and dated at the age of nine and the landscape in pencil showing exceptional talent at eleven are of especial interest since she began signing her drawings with her full name or with the initials H. B. P. when she was about ten years old.

Born in London on July 28, 1866, Beatrix Potter never went to school but was taught at home by governesses under whose sympathetic guidance during her teens the drawings reproduced here under the heading of Early Work were done. Shortly before her fifteenth birthday she received an Art Student's Certificate from the Science and Art Department of the Committee of Council on Education. This certificate, dated July 1, 1881, certifies that in freehand drawing, practical geometry, linear perspective and model drawing Helen B. Potter was of Second Grade.

From that time onward she seems to have kept on drawing whatever interested her wherever she was, investing each subject with reality. The power to give life, colour and texture to the inanimate is found to be increasingly pronounced throughout this period.

The selective skill and the grouping by subject which give form, coherence and cumulative interest to the first part of this book which adds a new dimension to the name of Beatrix Potter is fully sustained in the second part—Her Art in Relation to Her Books. Here under Imaginary Happenings in the Animal World, we find such enchanting fantasies as the Rabbits' Christmas Party, the Christmas Dinner (for Mice), the Guinea Pigs Go Gardening.

Beatrix Potter at play with rabbits, mice and guinea pigs begins also to play with ideas for illustrated books. Three Little Mice

Sat Down to Spin, and six drawings for Uncle Remus appear among others under Early Ideas for Illustrated Books.

Picture-Letters, to which the origin of her own writing and illustrating for children may be directly traced, are represented by a letter about Squirrel Nutkin. Comparison of this letter with the pictures and text of *The Tale of Squirrel Nutkin* gives an insight into Beatrix Potter's treatment from an idea to the finished book. Her search for the right word was as carefully determined as her choice of the right sketch to put into each picture.

Derwent Water is the setting for *Squirrel Nutkin* and the two background water-colours, on pages 208 and 210, were taken from a sketchbook in which all the Nutkin scenery is recorded. The original Squirrel Nutkin Story-Letter was sent to Norah Moore and is reproduced on pages 192 to 207.

Norah's sister, Freda, was the happy recipient of *The Tailor of Gloucester*. The story was written in a stout exercise book, with the water colour paintings pasted in, and sent with a letter of dedication which appeared in the published book in 1903. Since of all her books *The Tailor of Gloucester* was Beatrix Potter's favourite and contains some of her best work, the frontispiece for this book has been chosen from it.

Her books are presented in the order of their publication. With the reproductions from the original full scale drawings are shown also duplicate originals which were not used and many preliminary studies of exceptional interest. The reproduction from original drawings for her books, most important in their restoration of full colour values, are all significant in tracing a detail of background or incident to a sketch or a drawing made years before the picture for a particular book was painted.

To those who have known Beatrix Potter's books from childhood and have shared them with children, turning these pages becomes a veritable treasure hunt for the familiar and a fresh discovery of the artist herself.

For the young artist and designer of picture books *The Art of*

Beatrix Potter is an inexhaustible source of inspiration and a constant reminder of the good draughtsmanship she admired and insisted upon.

" Illustrators soon begin to go down hill," she wrote to her publishers in reply to a suggestion that she might illustrate other work than her own. " I will stick to doing as many as I can of my own books."

Since it was Mr. Herring who saw every one of the Beatrix Potter books through the press, it is most fortunate that his judgement and experience in the reproduction of her published work could be extended also to the hitherto unpublished work of this volume. I met Mr. Herring for the first time at the offices of Frederick Warne & Co. in London, in 1921. He was then seeing through the press a very beautiful book, *Kate Greenaway's Pictures* from originals presented by her to her friends. Later I was to learn from Leslie Brooke of the fine understanding and technical skill Mr. Herring had given to his picture books during the many years of Mr. Brooke's association with the House of Warne.

The series of excellent photographs which form the final section of *The Art of Beatrix Potter* were taken by Mr. Linder during the preparation of this volume which reflects his especial interest in books for young children and his admiration for an artist whose work he has studied intensively and felt a strong desire to preserve. Scenes made familiar by Jemima Puddle-duck, Tom Kitten, Duchess, of *The Pie and the Patty-pan*, and *The Roly-Poly Pudding* will be recognised in the photographs by those familiar with the pictures in the books.

For those who know and love the Lake Country the views of Hill Top and the surrounding countryside are a reminder of its quiet beauty and its hold on mind and heart. For those who have yet to discover the Lake District they provide a strong incentive for a rewarding pilgrimage to the home Beatrix Potter made for herself in the village of Sawrey.

" My brother and I were born in London," she once wrote, " but our descent, our interest and joy were all in the north country." Here the happiest years of her life were spent and when she died on December

22, 1943, as the wife of William Heelis, Hill Top Farm House with all the treasures she had so lovingly placed in it over the years was left to the National Trust of the United Kingdom with explicit directions for its arrangement and perpetual care.

Mr. Linder and Mr. Herring have not only paid a worthy tribute to Beatrix Potter as an artist, they have also added a record of compelling interest to children's books of the twentieth century. Whenever possible they have illuminated the record by reproduction of Beatrix Potter's comment in her own handwriting and by identification of the place where, and the date when, a drawing was made.

Since this record is also one of peculiar interest to American readers who have grown up with a sense of the importance of the continuity of English literature and art for children no less than for adult readers I have ventured to tell my own story of Beatrix Potter.

My story begins with the discovery of *The Tailor of Gloucester* among the new children's books sent over from London to an American children's library at Christmas-time 1903.

Far and few were the new books for little children at the turn of the century. Here was one of such exceptional quality and charm that it could be shared on equal terms with the head of the art department, with which this children's library was vitally connected, and the children to whom I first read it aloud in the children's room of the Pratt Institute Free Library in Brooklyn, New York. I have continued to read it every Christmas since then and it has lost none of its freshness as a work of art or as a Christmas story.

Enjoyment of books within the library itself was one of the main features of this children's library. The freedom from any restriction of age or custom gave parents as well as young children a natural free access to books in a homelike setting.

A children's library was a new idea and picture books played a major role in its development. The best ones obtainable from England, France and Germany were chosen to provide standards of excellence in art and incentives to the love of reading. Picture books which had hitherto been regarded as luxuries for those who could afford to buy them for their children were now seen to come alive in the same way in the hands of children from bookless homes and it became a thrilling experience to learn to see in a book what a child sees, regardless of his home environment.

I have always been glad that my own first impressions of Beatrix Potter as an artist were taken from *The Tailor of Gloucester* and from *Squirrel Nutkin*, published in the same year, rather than from *Peter Rabbit*. The individuality of character and setting of each little book remains clearer in mind in consequence and the value of her contribution to children's books, as her own direct communication of the natural world to children, more fully appreciated. To me they have always been Beatrix Potter's books rather than the Peter Rabbit books.

First visual impressions haunt the memory. I met Peter Rabbit for the first time in a hideous pirated American edition bearing all the stigmata of the new comic strip that was filling the vacuum before American publishers began to give any attention to the production of children's books as works of art. Peter Rabbit lent himself so readily to imitation, caricature and exploitation as a comic character as to obscure his importance to an educational world in which nature and art had been dead for a very long time. The important thing about Peter Rabbit was that he was alive and true to the nature of a rabbit, as was quickly recognised by the children as soon as the authorised English edition with Beatrix Potter's own pictures took its place in their library. Children who had never read before burst into reading as they turned the pages just as they did in hundreds of American homes where Peter Rabbit was taken to bed every night.

From the intimacy of daily association with children and their books in Brooklyn I went to New York, at the height of a fresh tide of immigration, to offer a similar natural free access to books, without age limit, in the children's rooms of The New York Public Library and its many branches. These were largely in foreign neighbourhoods but my confidence in picture books as first aids in creating a spontaneous desire to read was now firmly established. Picture books were indispensable.

With the opening of its impressive central building in 1911 the selection of picture books in the children's reading room attracted international interest, and the American children's library came to be regarded as " a new idea in education " for other countries. The first European library for children was opened in Stockholm the same year.

The First World War brought a shortage of picture books which called for serious measures of conservation on the part of the library. Children must not be deprived of enjoyment of the books but the life of each book must be prolonged by loving care and a renewed sense of its value on the part of everybody. The response of children and librarians was a wonderful tribute to the books of Caldecott, Kate Greenaway, Leslie Brooke and Beatrix Potter.

At the end of the war no visitor was more welcome than Mr. Fruing Warne, of Frederick Warne and Company, who came straight from the ship to the library and who brought good news of the reprinting of old favourites and the promise of new books from Beatrix Potter and Leslie Brooke. Then he told me that Beatrix Potter lived in the Lake District and that the illustrations for several of her books were from familiar scenes near her home, that the animals were all from living models—many of them her pets.

But when I asked where Beatrix Potter lived in the Lake District, Mr. Warne said that her publishers could give no personal information about her. " She is very averse to publicity of any kind," he said. " She is married now but continues to use her own name for her books. They have been remarkably successful. She has bought a farm from the royalties of *Peter Rabbit* and others." Mr. Warne had given me the first clue to the mystery of Beatrix Potter.

A year later I paid a return visit to Mr. Warne in Bedford Court, where he proved as gracious a host in London as he had been a visitor in New York, taking me behind the scenes to see new books in the making and to the shipping department to discover *Peter Rabbit* and *Benjamin Bunny* in French.

THE ART OF BEATRIX POTTER

I had just come from searching the bookshops of Paris for picture books for the children's libraries which had been opened in wooden *baraques* on the ruins of homes and schools in northern France. Picture books, good picture books, seemed more important than ever before and translations of those with universal appeal an imperative need of the time. That Beatrix Potter's publishers were recognising the importance of her work by translation was good news. Since *Pierre Lapin* and *Jeannot Lapin* were not yet available in France, I had the pleasure of ordering fifty copies to be sent to La Bibliothéque Populaire de Soissons, knowing well with what joy they would be received in the villages which were then being served by that library with the assistance of an American committee.

Before leaving Mr. Warne's office I told him that I was to spend the next fortnight in Grasmere and that I wished to write to Beatrix Potter from there introducing myself. " I can only wish you luck," Mr. Warne said but he gave me a slip of paper on which he had written Mrs. William Heelis, Sawrey, Ambleside. From the Moss Grove at Grasmere I wrote Mrs. Heelis a letter telling her of American children and French children and their love of picture books. I told her of my delight in finding *Pierre Lapin* and *Jeannot Lapin* in London and I spoke of some beautiful photographs of French children and their grandmothers looking at picture books together. Would she like to see the pictures ? By return post came the following letter :

June 24, 1921

Dear Miss Moore,
 We shall be very glad to see you. Can you come for lunch on Monday ? It is not a long notice but a pity to miss fine weather and we have not much hay cut at present. I wonder how you will get here ? (Two pages of explicit directions follow with an offer to send to the Ferry should I choose to come by boat.)
 Excuse a scribble, I have just come out of the hay. It is uncommonly warm.

Yours sincerely,
Beatrix Heelis

I like the French translations, it is like reading someone else's book— refreshing !

AN APPRECIATION

On that beautiful June morning I chose to walk up the long hill leading from the Ferry to the village of Sawrey. Wild roses were blooming in the hedgerows and the air was fragrant with new-mown hay. And suddenly, just as I had hoped she might, Beatrix Heelis came " out of the hay " to greet me, looking for all the world as Beatrix Potter should look. She was wearing a broad-brimmed straw hat and she carried a rake in her hand. On her feet were Lancashire clogs with buckles. Her sturdy figure was dressed for the hay field and not for company. Her bright blue eyes sparkled with merriment and her smile was that of a child who shares a secret, as indeed she did. She spoke with the tang of the north country. No welcome could have been more cordial than hers to Hill Top Farm. Beatrix Heelis was in the mid-fifties at that time but her cheeks were as rosy as those of a young girl and her eyes as clear and expectant.

Long before we came to the top of the lane leading to Castle Cottage I felt as if I had known her always. The familiar flower garden of her picture books tempted us to linger there, for the foxgloves were in their glory. " But it's time for lunch," said my hostess. " Mr. Heelis likes to be on time." William Heelis, tall and gentle in manner, with the ease of a man who belonged to that countryside, had just come from his law office in Ambleside.

I have no recollection of anything we ate or talked about at that mid-day meal but I was conscious of a fine reserve of quiet humour on the part of Mr. Heelis. He showed no surprise, but looked amused, when his wife turned to me with an expectant look and said, " If Mr. Heelis would drive you to Bowness afterward, couldn't you stay on for tea ? It would give more time to look about." I needed no urging to " stay on."

Looking about began with feeding Emily and Tapioca, leaders of a large family of turkeys, descendants of Charles the rooster, Pigling Bland and others. It meant seeing Hill Top Farm as Jemima Puddle-duck and Tom Kitten saw it.

Fascinating as it was to follow the farmyard trails with Beatrix

Potter herself, the best was yet to come when from her study in Castle Cottage she brought out one portfolio after another and left me free to browse at will among the pencil sketches, pen and ink drawings, the crayons, the water colours from which the pictures in her books had grown. " I can see that you are enjoying yourself," she said. " My portfolios are not in order but I can always find what I'm looking for when I need it. You may choose any one you think your children in New York would like."

When I chose a small water colour of rabbits playing in the snow with their sleds, Beatrix Potter was reminded of sitting out in the scorching summer sunshine painting snow scenes for *The Tailor of Gloucester*. I was absorbed in a portfolio of wild flowers—bluebells, primroses, daisies—when my hostess left me for an hour. When she came back she brought a portfolio of the fungi drawings. " I know these are good," she said quietly. " I made a great many of them, hoping they might illustrate a book I was not qualified to write. It needed a scientist. Some of the funguses are very rare. They made a fascinating study for a number of years. My eyes no longer permit me to do such fine work. I did enjoy finding them and painting them and they give me pleasure whenever I take time to look at them and recall the places they came from. The drawings fill seven portfolios and were done years before any of my books for children."

Admiration for the exquisite water colours, revealing the eye of the naturalist for each individual species and the feeling of the artist for the beauty and faery-like quality of the subject, led me to ask if she had ever exhibited her work. " No," Beatrix Potter replied. " I have never cared to exhibit my work. Very few people have ever seen the funguses. I am happy to know that you appreciate them." There was barely time to visit the dairy and watch Beatrix Heelis skim rich yellow cream for the strawberries which lent colour and fragrance to our tea. Nowhere out of the Lake District would one find such a tea.

Behind the tea-pot, with Mr. Heelis across the table, Beatrix Heelis turned to me, eyes sparkling with fun, and whispered, " If you had a nightie and toothbrush, couldn't you stay all night ? " Still dazed by all I'd seen that afternoon, I suddenly realised that the visit had turned into an adventure for Beatrix Potter herself as well as for me. I looked in vain for some sign of dissent or disapproval from Mr. Heelis who must have heard the whisper. " I think the nicest way of having company is to ask them to stay on after they come instead of before," Mrs. Heelis continued. " You haven't seen the half of Hill Top and I want to look at the French pictures again and hear more about the New York children. Please stay with us."

Who could resist such an invitation ? As we rose from the tea-table it was Beatrix Potter who handed me a huge door key. The key to her own Hill Top Farm House. " Now, run on down the lane and unlock the door and *rummage* to your heart's content and you'll be able to tell the children in New York that you've seen every nook and corner of Tom Kitten's House. You'll not be disturbed by any of Samuel Whiskers' relations. Enjoy yourself ! "

And so I entered Hill Top Farm House alone and found it exactly as it is pictured in *The Roly-Poly-Pudding*—the kitchen chimney up which Tom Kitten jumped, the cupboard where Moppet and Mittens were shut, the staircase on which Mrs. Tabitha Twitchit pattered up and down, the very same carpet and curtains, the mysterious attic where Ribby and Tabitha heard the roly-poly noise. I opened doors, peeked into cupboards and chests until I began to hear roly-poly noises myself. Then it was I discovered one after another the things Beatrix Potter had put into other books, the clock on the staircase, a chair in *The Tailor of Gloucester*, the very teacups the mice had peeped out from under, a wonderful old dresser. I explored the house all over again for signs of her own daily life there before she became Beatrix Heelis, and the house responded, as old houses will sometimes when one is quite alone and receptive.

As I locked the door and stepped into the lane, it was not of " Samuel Whiskers and his wife on the run with the wheel-barrow,"

I was thinking but of Beatrix Potter herself. She seemed as completely identified with the old house as with the pictures I had seen in the portfolios. In giving me freedom to explore both myself, she had given me friendship and trust.

We took a long walk with Mr. Heelis after that and watched the sun go down behind the Langdales from the top of the hill. Then back to Castle Cottage for a hot supper cooked by Beatrix Heelis herself.

The photographs of French children and their grandmothers enjoying pictures together led to many questions. Beatrix Potter had never been in France. " I've never been out of the British Isles," she said. When I told her of the old women I had seen who had chosen to live on in the ruins of their homes on their own land rather than take shelter with relatives or friends in the city, she exclaimed, " That is just what I should do if my home was destroyed—stay on the land."

Pictures of children looking at picture books, pictures of children listening to stories in France or in New York libraries, pictures of children making their own free choice of books from the shelves of public libraries excited her interest and wonder as something new and strange.

We visited the " Ginger and Pickles " shop together next morning and before I went on my way we stopped at Hill Top Farm House where Beatrix Heelis inscribed a copy of *The Roly-Poly Pudding* with my name " from ' Beatrix Potter ' in remembrance of Hill Top Farm, Sawrey, June 27, 1921." It is the edition of larger size in which the book was first published.

" You will always be welcome at Hill Top whenever you come to England," she said, " and you may send any of the storytellers in your children's libraries. I know they would be coming for the sake of the children and not out of mere curiosity."

It was in May, 1937, after the Coronation celebrations in London, that I came to Hill Top again for a visit as memorable as, but entirely different from, the first round-the-clock one of 1921.

" It will be a pleasure and an interesting event to see you again," Beatrix Heelis had written on May 4th. " I wish you had been here this week—the country has been looking so lovely—cherry blossom, whitethorn, damson all out in bloom together. . . . The bluebells will be out next week. . . . The hawthorns will be very fine ; buds just showing. I will show you the Troutbeck woods if we have time. . . . I can send to meet the 5.15 at Windermere an old-fashioned black and green Talbot saloon and an aged chauffeur. We hope for a very fine pleasant visit this time."

Whoever knows England at Coronation time will recall the after-glow of the great day in the villages. It still lingered in Sawrey. Beatrix Heelis, radiant at seventy, welcomed me in holiday mood. This time she came out of her Pringle Wood to tell me the bluebells were in bloom. The hedgerows were white with hawthorn, lilacs scented the air, and every garden in the village was bright with tulips and late daffodils.

There was much to talk about during the long first evening. Our sixteen-year-old friendship had been kept warm by exchange of letters and books at Christmas-time and at other times. Beatrix Heelis had bought one farm after another beyond the boundaries of Hill Top during those years. She had become a widely respected and honoured sheep farmer of the north country. Had her interest in Herdwick sheep completely absorbed Beatrix Potter the creative artist ? If her letters had left a doubt it would have been dispelled by the talk of this evening and of days that followed.

" I want to show you the farms which have the most beautiful views," she said. " We'll take a drive every morning, rain or shine." And so to Skelwith, Coniston, Little Langdale we were driven by the aged chauffeur who sat patiently waiting while we looked about old farms and cottages which seemed a part of the landscape.

The high point for me on that wonderful guided tour of the Lake District was reached at Troutbeck Park Farm where a sheep shearing was going on outside and a knot of shepherds had gathered from neighbouring farms. Mrs. Heelis regarded her sheep with an appraising eye to their condition after a hard winter. Few words were spoken but she exchanged greetings with each one of the shepherds and mingled with them to watch the shearing.

Inside the Shepherd's cottage, high above the old-fashioned open cooking stove, hung a very large oil painting of sheep in the Scottish Highlands. " It is one of my brother's paintings," said Beatrix Heelis, " It was too large for the room I set apart at Hill Top for his pictures. The Shepherd's wife seems to enjoy having it here. She says it gives her a lift to look as far as Scotland when she feels she has too much to do."

When I spoke of a fine old chest in another room of the cottage, Beatrix Heelis gave it a loving pat. " I cannot resist the old oak cupboards and chests at an auction so I buy them and fit them in wherever I can."

Troutbeck Park Farm stands at the head of the long curving Troutbeck Valley. Beyond it tower High Street and Ill Bell. I had often passed the lonely farm on my walks on the fells in the summer of 1906, the very summer Beatrix Potter was getting Hill Top Farm House ready to live in.

At the other end of the Valley stands Town End, the house of an old statesman family, handed down from father to son from the Elizabethan age. It was there I had spent many happy months and had learned from its owner, a retired sheep farmer who had won many medals for his Herdwick sheep, a great deal about the Lake District and its people, for Mr. George Browne was an antiquarian who cherished his inheritance and took great pride in keeping his ancestral home unchanged.

" We could stop at Town End if you like," said Beatrix Heelis. " Miss Clara Browne is still living there I am told. I have never been inside the house. Would you care to see it again ? " I hesitated, it was twenty-five years since I last stayed there, but I realised Beatrix Heelis would really like to see it. The ancient " house-place " in whose restoration Mr. Browne had taken such pride was just as he had left it. And while Beatrix Heelis looked around, I stole upstairs to find that the mysterious little oak writing room, which opened into my bedroom, was still there.

That evening our talk was all of Troutbeck. It was then that Beatrix Heelis told me of her wanderings over Troutbeck fell, of the dance of the wild fell ponies about the thorn tree. " It was finding their little fairy foot-marks on the old drove road that first made me aware of the Fairy Caravan," she said. She had wandered farther into the wilderness behind Troutbeck Tongue than I had, but for each of us as we had walked alone, without loneliness, there remained a memory of complete enchantment.

On Saturday Mr. Heelis took a holiday and drove us to Hawkshead where he unlocked the door of the old Grammar School. Wordsworth attended this school and was possibly its most famous pupil. Mr. Heelis showed us the Letters Patent granted to the school by Queen Elizabeth I in 1585. He also showed us the old cottages of special interest for their human associations. I realised more fully that day how much Beatrix Potter must have learned from William Heelis about that countryside.

" You would like to see Buttermere again, wouldn't you ? " Beatrix Heelis said on Sunday morning. " It's a rare day and there is a little matter of business to take me there. Let's make a day of it, Willie ! "

What a glorious day it is to recall ! Beatrix Heelis seated comfortably on the back seat " with room to spread out." William Heelis driving with the ease of one enjoying the countryside and quite ready to stop for a view at any moment. Over Brathay Bridge, through Ambleside, past Rydal Water to Grasmere, where we lingered for some time; then on past Thirlmere to Keswick, still gaily decorated for the Coronation, and Derwentwater.

Between Keswick and Cockermouth we stopped for a leisurely luncheon at the Golden Pheasant and took a rest by feasting our eyes on the primrose banks of a lovely stream. Few words were spoken the whole day long. It was a day of utter contentment in a world of beauty.

We came to Buttermere at last and to the farm at the foot of Honister Pass, and while Beatrix Heelis attended to her little matter of business, Mr. Heelis and I left the car to climb higher for another view.

On the way home we stopped for tea at a cottage under Helvellyn and again at the tiny church at Wytheburn. There was another pause at Grasmere, for the evening light on the hills was very beautiful and Grasmere, like Troutbeck, had memories we shared.

Beatrix Potter rested in the afternoons and on one of them I explored Pringle Wood for signs of Pony Billy on " the fairy hill of oaks." " How blue the bluebells were : a sea of soft pale blue ; tree behind tree ; and beneath the trees, wave upon wave, a blue sea of bluebells."

On another day I wandered through Codlin Croft orchard with *The Fairy Caravan* and came back to read with fresh delight the conversation between Charles the cock and the hens, Selina Pickacorn, Tappie-tourie and Chucky-doddie. Re-reading *The Fairy Caravan* at Hill Top led me to speak of its richness and variety, of its true relation to each one of the little books. " It puts the very life of the England they came out of behind them and it gives Beatrix Potter her own place in it," I said. " You did not mention it when I was here before."

" No, at that time I thought of it as too personal to be of interest to anyone else," Beatrix Heelis replied. " I am very slow about making up my mind about things. It takes years sometimes for an idea to take shape. It was so with several of the books—years between a picture-letter idea and the book. When I look back I realise it was Miss Bertha Mahony, of the Bookshop in Boston, with her questions about Beatrix Potter and how she came to write and illustrate *Peter Rabbit* and the others, who set me thinking outside myself. I found her questions very perplexing at the time and I sent a short answer, through my publishers, telling her very little she wanted to know."

Miss Mahony had also fortunately sent Beatrix Potter copies of the magazine she was editing, the Horn Book, a magazine devoted to children's books which carried a reproduction of a drawing from Caldecott's *Three Jovial Huntsmen* on the cover. Beatrix Potter was pleased that Caldecott was being remembered in America.

" I have always had the greatest admiration for Caldecott as an artist," she said. " At one time I tried in vain to copy him. We had all his picture books as they came out and my father bought many of his original drawings at a sale after Caldecott's death."

" I found the Horn Book pleasantly written and in good taste. Gradually I began to see a reason for Miss Mahony's questions. She was very tactful and did not press them but she kept on sending the magazine and I continued to read it for about two years."

" Then I had a problem I thought she might understand. I wanted to help save that strip of land on the shore of Windermere—we stopped there for the beautiful view on our way home from Trout-beck. I had given all the money I could afford to the fund that was being raised for the purpose. And so I wrote a letter to Miss Mahony with the assistance of Peter Rabbit, and offered to send an autographed drawing in return for a contribution of a guinea to the fund. She reproduced my letter in the Horn Book (August, 1927) and gave it a title, ' Peter Rabbit and his Homelands.' The Bookshop quickly sold the fifty drawings I sent. That was the beginning of my personal correspondence with Bertha Mahony."

There were many American visitors to Hill Top after that letter appeared. Two of them wrote of their visits in the Horn Book. One of them, a twelve-year-old boy from Boston, gave a circumstantial account of his visit in which he mentioned seeing in Beatrix Potter's portfolios " Unpublished pictures just as fascinating as those printed in the books."

It was he who discovered the unfinished story of guinea pigs which became the first chapter in *The Fairy Caravan* and it is to him, Henry

P., the book is dedicated. The other visitor was Miss Helen Dean Fish, editor of children's books for a New York publishing house, who told Beatrix Heelis that *The Tailor of Gloucester* had always been her favourite among the little books. This was welcome news from a discriminating American editor who wrote of Hill Top out of the deep feeling for England which had made her a contributor to the National Trust.

Bertha Mahony made a happy choice of words when she renewed an early request and asked for the " roots " of Beatrix Potter and her books. Her letter brought the reply for which she had waited patiently and expectantly for four years. Under the title *The Roots of the Peter Rabbit Tales, by Beatrix Potter*, it was published in the Horn Book in the same year the first chapter of the *The Fairy Caravan* appeared there under the title *Over the Hills and Far Away*. The book was first published in Philadelphia in 1929.

" I should never have dared to risk the book without Miss Mahony's belief in its interest for those who have cared for my work. It required a personal visit from an American publisher to bring about its publication there, to be sure, but I should never have consented to part with it if I had not been told it was wanted and needed to complete my story of England and my books which had seemed so trivial for so many years on both sides of the Atlantic.

" Bertha Mahony Miller and I have never met, yet I feel that I know her very well as a person, we like so many of the same things. I am glad she has kept on with the Horn Book since her marriage. The Bookshop she originated had to go. One cannot keep on with everything. But one never gives up a real interest in children or ' a firm belief in fairies '," she added with a lovely smile.

The visit lasted nearly a week and there was time for good talk of books other than her own, time to explore her bookshelves and discover how varied her book interests had been. " I have been thinking of the importance of saving books as well as scenery," she said one day. " Books are soon lost or forgotten and children's books are the most perishable of all. It makes me happy to feel mine are being saved in libraries overseas."

Little did we dream that another war would so soon threaten the lives of picture books in every country. That American libraries would again be put to the test of conserving for the future while heeding the call of the present generation to see what a country is like from its picture books. Beautiful picture books had come to the children's libraries in the 1920's—from Italy, Sweden, Holland, Poland, Czechoslovakia and other countries.

The remarkable development of picture books conceived and produced as works of art by publishers in America, which began during the same decade, was greatly stimulated by seeing the foreign picture books in the hands of children who also delighted in the books of Walter Crane, Randolph Caldecott, Kate Greenaway and Boutet de Monvel. Language is no barrier to enjoyment of a picture book in which the artist conveys true impressions of his country to children.

Beatrix Potter was interested in the development of picture books in America. The freedom for experiment in technique and methods of reproduction appealed to her. "There is bound to be a waste to arrive at anything worth while," she said. "No doubt American artists and publishers will find that out in time, with the help of the children."

In her letters during the war years she often spoke of children's books. In response to a copy of *To Think That I Saw It on Mulberry Street*, she wrote, "I think it the cleverest book I have met with for many years. The swing and merriment of the pictures and the natural truthful simplicity of the untruthfulness . . . Too many story books for children are condescending, self-conscious inventions—and then some trival oversight, some small incorrect detail gives the whole show away. Dr. Seuss does it thoroughly."

"It is very interesting to read about the beginnings—like St. Nicholas. I had it to read but not in the earliest days. I had the *Silver Skates*, which I have unfortunately lost. I have most of Mrs. Ewing's and Mrs. Molesworth's books—very old copies carefully kept. They were as good as the American books but less humorous . . . I have been re-reading *Huckleberry Finn*."

" Let us hope for peace before another New Year," she wrote in conclusion to this letter of 1940. " But we will just stick it out whatever happens . . . People take it calmly, with temper, not fear. The sheep and cattle take no notice."

For three more years she continued to write with an eye undimmed for the beauty of her countryside and a faith unshaken by fear of invasion or destruction. Facing the red glare in the sky of Liverpool and Manchester burning, she could say, " If it were not for pity one might say it was a fine sight."

Anne Carroll Moore

PART 1

BEATRIX POTTER—THE ARTIST

1

EARLY WORK (1876-1882)

Beatrix Potter   Age 9

Helen Beatrix Potter. Feb 9. 1876.

Flower Drawing   Age 9 years, 6 months

Landscape

Age 11 years, 3 months

Age 14

Carnations

September 27th 1880

Age 14

Bramble Leaves

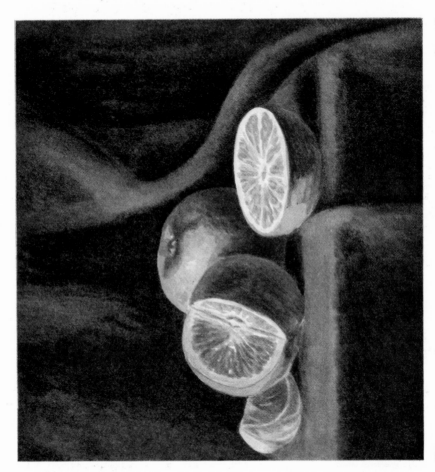

Age 16

Oranges

Age 17

Grapes and Peaches

Vase of Daffodils

Early Sketches

Wray Castle   Age 16

2

INTERIORS (*1882-1903*)

" A Winter Evening "

" Old house at Winchelsea, Sussex "

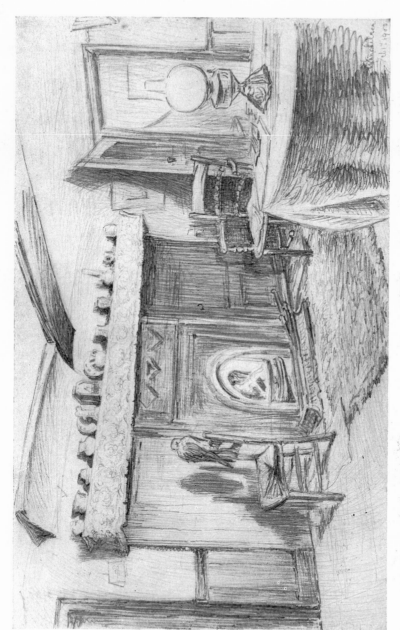

Feb. 1st, 1900

In an old house at Winchelsea

In an old house at Winchelsea   Feb. 2nd, 1900

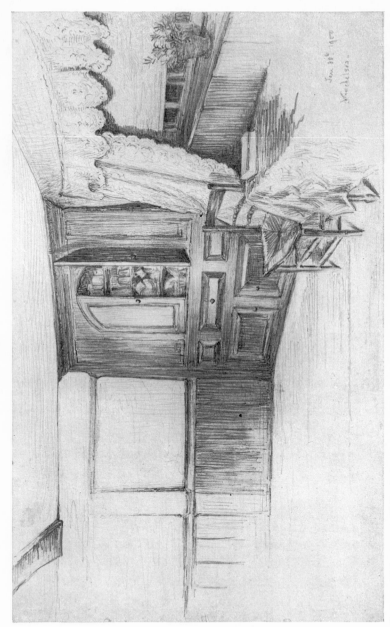

Jan. 30th, 1900

In an old house at Winchelsea

In an old house at Winchelsea

In an old house at Winchelsea

In an old house at Winchelsea

Bedwell Lodge, near Hatfield September, 1891

√28361

Bedroom, Camfield Place, Hatfield, Herts

" No. 4 where I always slept. After my grandmother's death I asked for
the bedstead with green hangings—the chairs, the looking glass and 8 pictures
were given me. I still have them—also the Alabaster figure of Ariadne riding
the leopard, which was under a glass shade on the mantelpiece. The red
bed quilt also I used many years at B. Gardens."

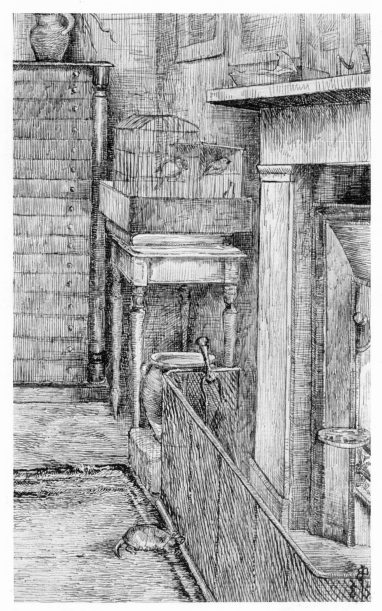

Corner of School Room   2, Bolton Gardens, Nov. 26th, 1885

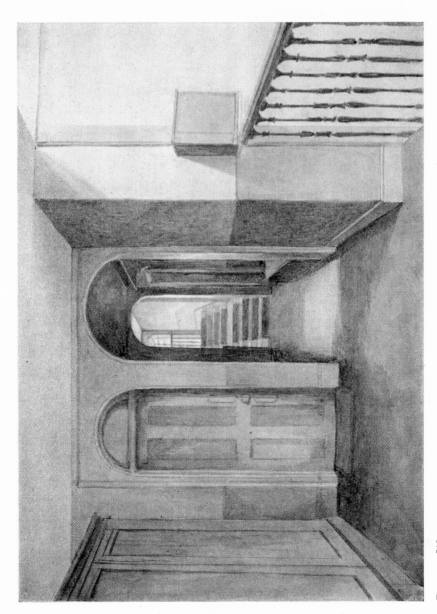

Passage Way

Lingholm, Keswick

Gwaynynog, Denbigh, Wales

'Gwaynynog, Denbigh   " A Welsh dresser, date 1696 "
                                              Feb. 1903

Melford Hall, Suffolk   (Unfinished)

Melford Hall, Suffolk

(About 1902)

A page from her Sketch Book

Interior of a Room   January, 1900 (Unfinished)

Spiral Staircase

Sketches made at Winchelsea   February, 1900

An old Barn   September, 1891

Interior of a Barn   October, 1891

The grinding Mill

3

HOUSES, VILLAGE SCENES
AND LANDSCAPE

August 15th 1884

House on the Lee, near Hatfield   August, 1884

House on the Lee, near Hatfield   September, 1884

House on the Lee, near Hatfield   Summer, 1884

Steps to the Bowling Green house, Melford Hall, Suffolk

Melford Hall, Suffolk

Melford Hall, Suffolk

Melford Hall, Suffolk

" A Hertfordshire Farm," Hatfield   Sept. 23rd, 1910

" On the road to Bury St. Edmunds "   Long Melford, Suffolk

" An old Mill on the Stour "   Suffolk

Amersham, Bucks

Aug. 30th, 1905

Aug. 3rd, 1905

Old Market House, Amersham, Bucks

Lyme Regis, Dorset

Lyme Regis, Dorset

"A Sheltered Cot"

Landscape   Oct. 1st, 1911

Helm Farm, near Windermere   April 13th, 1900

July, 1902

Laund House Farm, Bolton Abbey

Laund House, Bolton Abbey
(July 2nd to July 8th 1902)

A page from her Sketch Book

" A Beechwood near Inver, Dunkeld "   June, 1892

Woodland Sketch

Sept. 27th, 1899

Kirkcudbright Bay, Scotland

Forest Scene

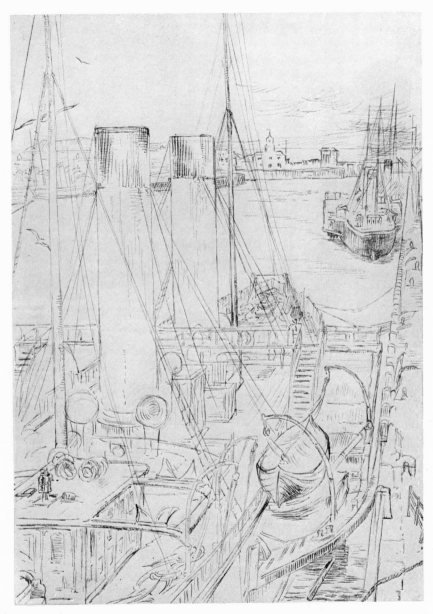

The Paddle Steamer, Holyhead   May, 1889

4

GARDENS, PLANT STUDIES
AND STILL LIFE

Garden Porch

Lingholm, Keswick

" An English Garden," Lakefield, Sawrey (now " Ees Wyke ")

Water Lilies

" Spring "

Study of a Carnation   Aug. 23rd, 1903

Flower Study

Flower Study   Aug, 26th, 1903

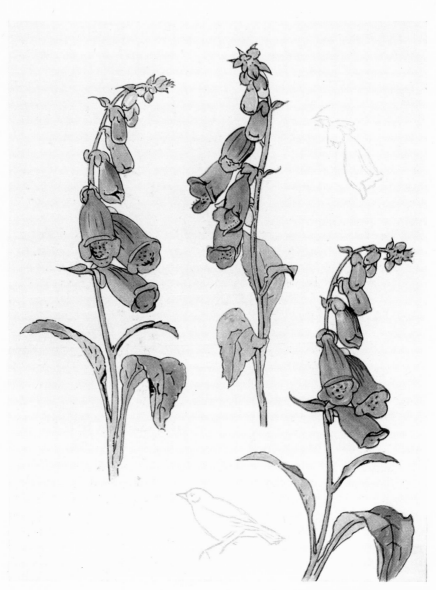

Foxgloves

Sidmouth, April 16th, 1902

" Blossomed Furze "

Broad Beans   Sept. 1st, 1903

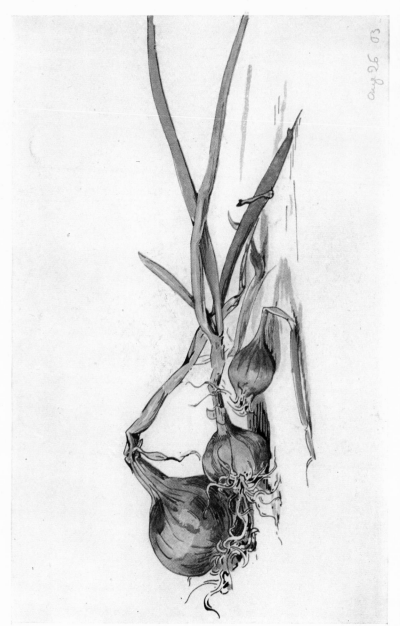

Aug. 26th, 1903

Onions

Blackcurrant

Elderberry

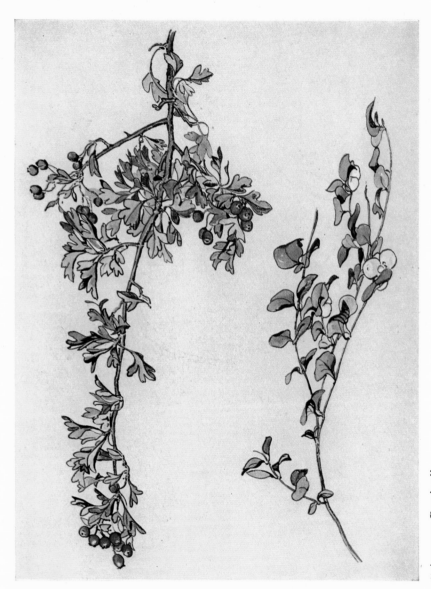

" Autumn Berries "

Oak Leaves

Wild Flowers

Leaf Design

April, 1900

" A Study in Reds "

5

MICROSCOPIC WORK AND FUNGI DRAWINGS

Vanessa Cardui
Scales on lower side of wing highly magnified

Painted Lady Butterfly

Small Tortoise-shell Butterfly
Vanessa Urticae
Scales on upper side of wing highly magnified

Small Tortoise-shell Butterfly

Vanessa Urticae
Scales on upper side of wing highly magnified

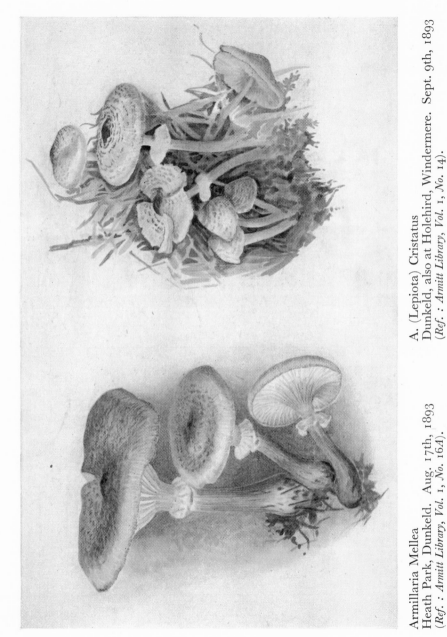

A. (Lepiota) Cristatus
Dunkeld, also at Holehird, Windermere. Sept. 9th, 1893
(Ref.: Armitt Library, Vol. 1, No. 14).

Armillaria Mellea
Heath Park, Dunkeld. Aug. 17th, 1893
(Ref.: Armitt Library, Vol. 1, No. 16A).

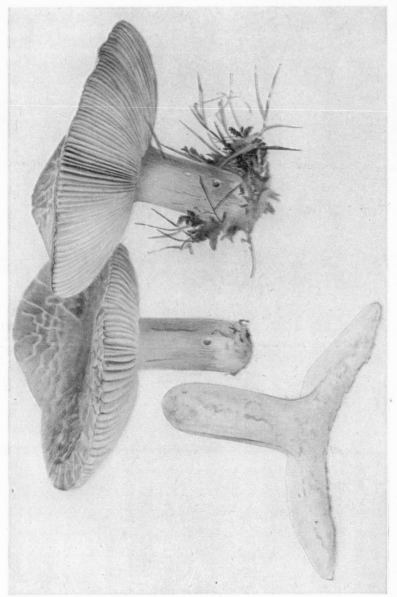

Hatchnize Wood, Coldstream. Aug. 3rd, 1894

Russula Lepida

(Ref. : Armitt Library, Vol. 2, No. 29).

A. (Lepiota) Granulosus

Tomgarrow Strath Braan
Oct. 8th, 1893

(Ref. : Armitt Library, Vol. 1, No. 13).

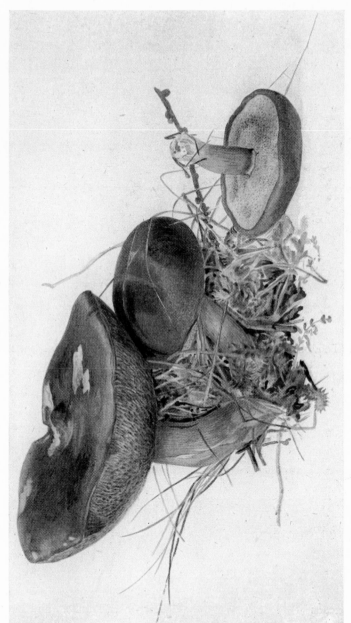

Boletus Badius

(*Ref.: Armitt Library, Vol. 6, No.* 139).

Fir Wood between Smailholm Tower and Kelso
Sept. 19th, 1894

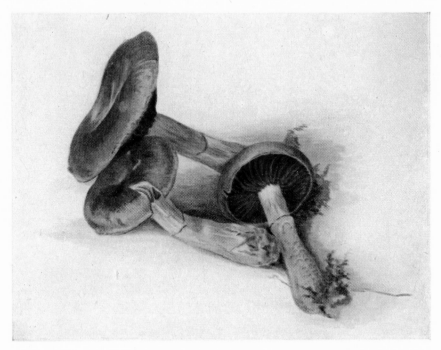

Cortinarius (Telamonia) Torvus   Dunkeld. Aug. 25th, 1893

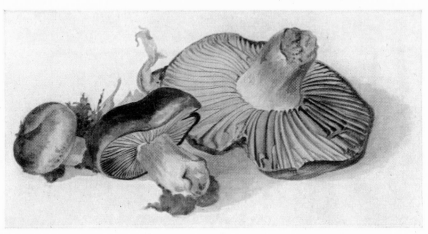

Russula Nigricans   Eastwood, Dunkeld and Lennel
                                      Aug. 28th, 1893

(Ref.: Armitt Library, Vol. 4, No. 109, and Vol. 2, No. 28).

6

ANIMAL STUDIES

Studies of a Bat   January, 1885

Weasel

Tortoise

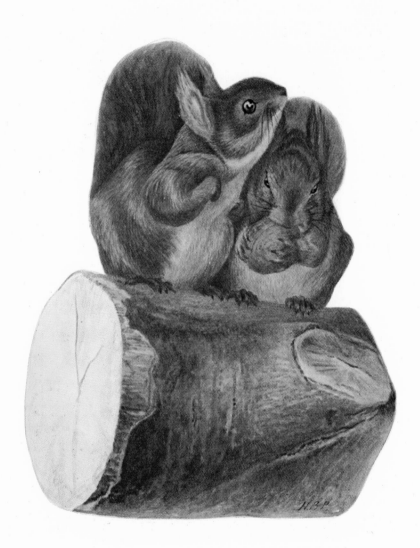

Squirrel Study

Squirrel Study

Squirrel Study

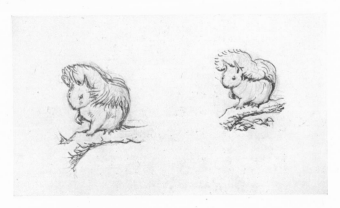

Squirrel Sketches

August, 1899

Peter Rabbit

" Peter Rabbit
he had an old quilt made of scraps
of flannel and blue cloth which
he always lay on "

Rabbits and Bird

Heads of Rabbits

A Mouse in its Nest

" Wood Mouse "   " Christmas 1886 "

Studies of Mice

Studies of Cats

Sketches of Pigs

Sheep and Cows

Heads of Rams

Studies of Cows

Farmyard Sketches

March 5th, 1909

"Kep" The Sheep Dog

PART 2

BEATRIX POTTER—HER ART
IN RELATION TO HER BOOKS

7

IMAGINARY HAPPENINGS IN THE ANIMAL WORLD

A RABBITS' CHRISTMAS PARTY

The Arrival

The Meal

After the Meal

The Departure

The Rabbit's Dream

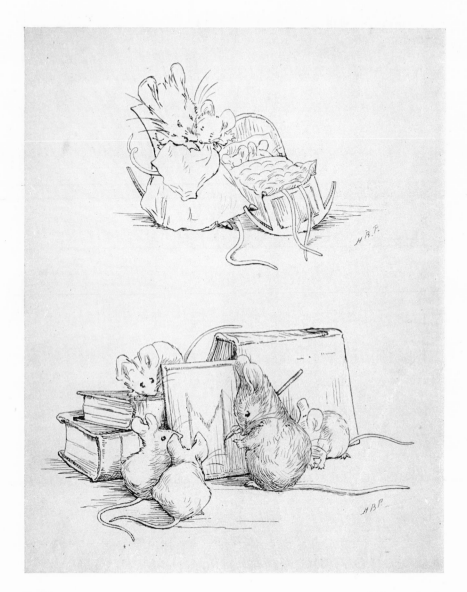

Bedtime   (About 1893)

Learning to Read

" This old mouse is teaching its children to read, you see it has made a big M on the slate "

The Rabbits' Potting Shed

The Mice in their Storeroom

" The peculiar Dream of Mr. Samuel Whiskers "

The Christmas Dinner   Dec. 1893

Mrs. Mouse goes Shopping

" Sparrows are CHEAP today "

(Rough sketch)

Sketch of a Rabbits' Party   (Rough sketch)

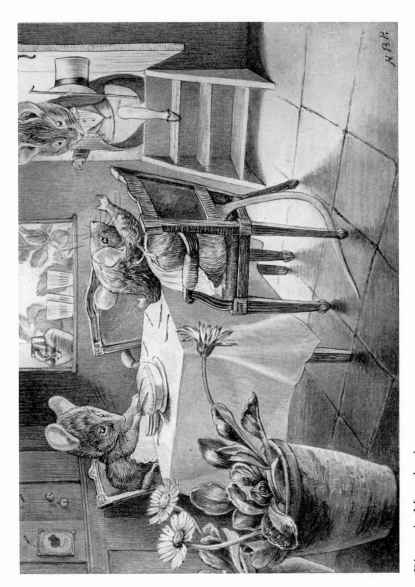

Dinner in Mouseland

The Guinea-pigs go Gardening

The day's News

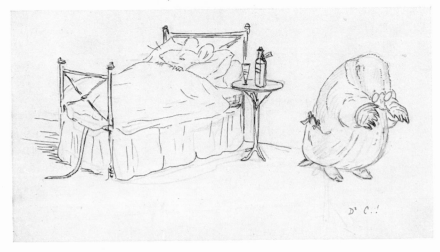

A visit from the Doctor

8

EARLY IDEAS FOR ILLUSTRATED BOOKS

A Preliminary Sketch for "A Happy Pair," to illustrate
a set of verses

One of the illustrations for "A Happy Pair,"
the first of her work to be published. (About 1890)

Design for a Book Cover, or Title Page   June 1894

"I have brought you, sire, this rabbit, from the warren of my lord the marquis of Carabas, who commanded me to present it to your majesty, with the assurance of his respect."

A SERIES OF DRAWINGS TO ILLUSTRATE
" UNCLE REMUS "

" Brer Fox and Brer Rabbit "   1893

"Is de dogs all gone, Brer Rabbit?"
"Seem like I hear one un um
smellin' roun' de chimbly-cornder
des now."........
"Wat dat I hear, Brer Rabbit?"
"You hear de win' a blowin', Brer
Wolf."

" The awful fate of Mr. Wolf "   March, 1895

May, 1895

" Brer Rabbit rescues the Terrapin or Tortoise "

" Ole Mr. Benjamin Ram keep on chunin' up—Plank!—Plink!—Plunk!—
Plank! Miss Wolf drap her knife an' listen— "

Sept. 1895

Mr Benjamin Ram, going to play the fiddle at a ball, loses his way.
He discovers too late that he has asked for shelter at a house inhabited
by wolves. They receive him effusively & promise him a good supper,
but he hears them sharpening a knife. He thinks he will play
a last tune on his fiddle, the wolves are completely puzzled, & bolt—
Original, drawn by   Beatrix Potter.

Brer Fox t'un 'im over, he did, 'en 'zamine 'im 'in say—
"Dish yer rabbit dead. He look like he bin dead
long time... He's de fattes' rabbit wat I ever see,
but he bin dead too long. I fear'd ter take 'im
home." sezee.

Brer Fox goes a-hunting, but Brer Rabbit bags the game   Nov. 1895

Brer Rabbit steals Brer Wolf's Fish   Jan. 1896

THREE LITTLE MICE SAT DOWN TO SPIN

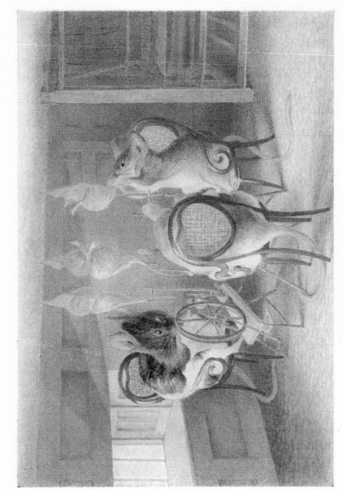

" Three little mice sat down to spin,

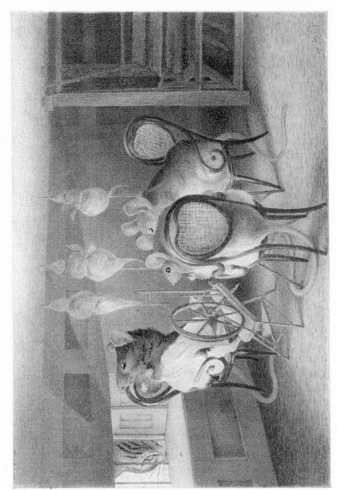

Pussy passed by and she peeped in.

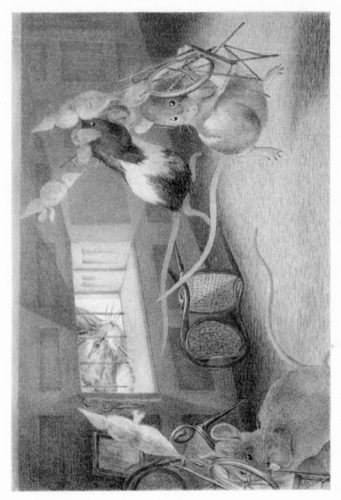

What are you at, my fine little men ?

Making coats for gentlemen.

"Shall I come in and cut off your threads ?
Oh, no, Miss Pussy, you'd bite off our heads !"

A Riddle

Ninny Nanny Netticoat
With a white
 petticoat
And a red nose—
The longer she stands
 The shorter she grows—

A Riddle . . . .

.... The Answer   August, 1897

Preliminary Sketch for " Toads'-tea-party "

If acorn cups were tea-cups
What should we have to drink ?
Oh honey-dew for sugar
In a cuckoo-pint of milk,
Set out upon a toadstool
On a cloth of cob-web silk,
With pats of witches' butter
And a tansey cake, I think !

Toads'-tea-party

A Cinderella Fantasy

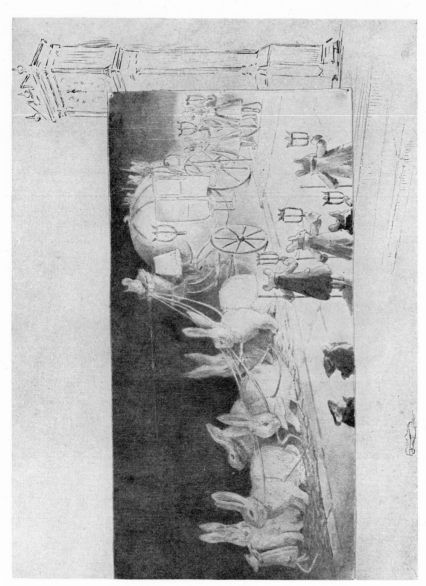

Cinderella's Carriage

"That is Not a
fat pigeon"

" The Fox and the Grapes "

The Fox and the Stork

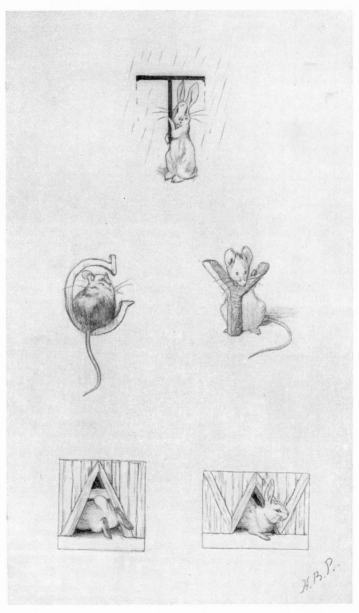

Designs for Letters of the Alphabet   (About 1893)

BEATRIX POTTER'S OWN COPY OF A STORY-LETTER
SENT TO ERIC MOORE

(An early version of " The Tale of Little Pig Robinson ")

Rosehmin Hotel
Falmouth
March 25. 94

My dear Eric

.. there are a great many ships here, some very large ones. there is one from Norway; and a French one unloading at the quay. Some of the sailors have little dogs, and cocks and hens on the ships. I have read about the owl & the pussy cat, who went to sea in a pea green boat, but I never saw anything of that kind till today.

I was looking at a ship called the Pearl of Falmouth which was being mended at the bottom because it had rubbed on a rock, when I heard something grunt!

I went up a bench where I could see onto the deck & there was a white pig with a curly tail walking about. It is a ship that goes to Newfoundland & the sailors always take a pig. I daresay it enjoys the voyage, but when the sailors get hungry they eat it. If that pig had any sense it would slip down into the boat at the end of the ship & row away.
This is the captain & the boatswain & the ship's cook pursuing the pig. The cook is waving a knife and fork. He wants

to make the pig into sausages!

This is the pig
rowing away from
the sailors, it is
squealing because it
sees the knife & fork.
This is the pig
living on Robinson
Crusoe's Island.
He is still
rather afraid of the Cook & is looking for the
ship through a telescope.
This is the same pig
after he has lived ten
years upon the island,
he has grown.
very very fat and the
Cook has never found him.

A LETTER TO A CHILD TELLING OF PETER RABBIT
AND OF OTHER ANIMAL FRIENDS

March 6th 97

My dear Walter

Thank you for your nice letter, but I am sorry to hear about poor Frisky. Another squirrel I knew died lately. It was a grey American squirrel and lived 8 or 9 years. The lady who had it says red squirrels do not live so well in cages as the grey ones,

Peter Rabbit is very well and fat,
generally asleep before the fire. On
Tuesday night there was a tremendous
wind and I went out
after dark and brought
him into the house.
Next morning the hutch was blown
right over; if he had
been inside he would have been hurt,
for the blue saucer was all in bits.

I have not heard much about Jack
lately but the owl is said to be a
great nuisance. Bertram has got
them with him in Scotland and
the owl hoots all night.
If he has a dead mouse
he bites it's head off and
then shouts as loud as he can.

An old woman gave Bertram a
present of 5 dozen eggs, rather too
many to eat. he sent them to us.
I have been drawing funguses very
hard, I think some day they will be

put in a book [sketch] but it will be a
dull one to read. We have had one
little fungus like red holly berries [sketch]
it had only been found once before in Scotland
I am glad you have got a nice dog, ours
had the cramp very [sketch] badly
in the cold weather; he falls down when
he is walking. We have got 4 canaries
I hope they will lay some eggs. [sketch]
[sketch] A friend of mine has got a
savage dormouse, it bites something
like the prick of a pin. It lost half
its tail by accident, it seems to have spoiled
its temper. I remain yr aff Cousin
Beatrix Potter.

A PICTURE-STORY ABOUT A GUINEA-PIG

The perfidious friend assures the guinea-pig it "won't hurt."

The guinea-pig has doubts—

but they are over-borne

The friend and the dentist take a professional interest in the *tooth*, but none whatever in the *victim*—

and go off discussing the successful operation

9

HER BOOKS—SOME PRELIMINARY SKETCHES AND FINISHED WORK

THE ART OF BEATRIX POTTER

PETER RABBIT (1902)

" Peter Rabbit's Fir Tree "

A preliminary Sketch for Frontispiece

" Rough Sketch "

Then old Mrs Rabbit took
a basket and her umbrella,
and went through the wood
to the baker's; she bought a
loaf of brown bread and 5
currant buns.

" Then old Mrs. Rabbit took a basket and her umbrella,
and went through the wood . . . "

*Original

*The term " Original " indicates that this drawing was the one reproduced
in the book.

BEATRIX POTTER'S FIRST VERSION OF "SQUIRREL NUTKIN"
(Sent to Norah Moore to whom the book was dedicated)

Lingholme, Keswick
Sept 25ᵗʰ 01.

My dear Norah,
There are such numbers of squirrels in the woods here. They are all very busy just now gathering nuts, which they hide away in little holes, where they can find them again, in the winter.

An old lady who lives on the island says she thinks they come over the lake when her nuts are ripe; but I wonder how they can get across the water? Perhaps

they make little rafts!

One day I saw a most comical
little squirrel; his tail was only an
inch long; but he was so impertinent,
he chattered and clattered

and threw

down acorns

onto my

head

I believe that his name was Nutkin
and that he had a brother called
Twinkleberry,
and this is
the story of how
he lost his tail — —
There is a big island in the
middle of the lake, covered with woods,
and in the middle of it stands
a hollow oak-tree which is the
house of an owl, called Old
Brown. One autumn when the
nuts were ripe, Nutkin and
Twinkleberry, and all the other

little squirrels came down to the
edge of the lake and paddled across
over the water to Owl Island to
gather nuts.   Each squirrel had
a little sack with him, and a
large oar, and spread out his tail
for a sail

They also carried with them an offering of 3 fat mice for Old Brown, which they placed upon a stone opposite his door.

Then Twinkleberry and the other squirrels each made a low bow,

and said politely — "Old Mr Brown,
will you favour us with permission
to gather nuts upon your island?"
. But Nutkin, who was excessively
impertinent in his manners, jumped
up + down, and shouted —
"Old Mr B.! riddle-me-ree?
Higgledy piggledy
  Here we lie,
Pick'd and pluck'd,
  And put in a pie:
My first is snapping, snarling, growling
My second's industrious, romping, prowling.
  Higgledy, piggledy,
  Here we lie,
  Pick'd and pluck'd
  And put in a pie!"
. . . .
Now this riddle is as old as the
hills. Mr Brown paid no attention
whatever to Nutkin.

The squirrels filled their bags and
sailed away home in the evening.

The next morning they all came
back again to Owl Island; and
Twinkleberry and the others brought
a fine fat mole, and laid it on
the stone in front of Old Brown's
door, and said —

"Mr Brown will you favour us
with your gracious permission to
gather some more nuts?"   But

Nutkin, who had no respect, danced
up & down and sang —
"Old Mr B! riddle-me-ree?
    As soft as silk,
    As white as milk,
As bitter as gall, a thick wall,
And a green coat covers me all!"
- - - - - - - - - -
Mr Brown made no reply to the
impertinent Nutkin.

On the 3rd day the squirrels came
back again and brought a present
of 7 fat minnows.

But Nutkin who had no manners
danced up & down, and sang —

" Old Mr B! riddle me ree?
As I came through the garden gap,
Who should I meet but Dick Red-cap,
A stick in his hand, a stone in his throat
If you'll tell me this riddle
I'll give you a groat!" — —

Which was very absurd of Nutkin,
because he did not possess 4 pence;
even if Mr Brown had taken the
trouble to answer.

The fourth day the squirrels came
with a present of 6 large beetles for
old Brown. But Nutkin
danced up and down
and sang as rudely as
ever —

"Old Mr B! riddle-me-ree?
Flour of England, fruit of Spain,
Met together in a shower of rain;
Put in a bag tied round with a string,
If you'll tell me this riddle,
I'll give you a ring!"
- - - - - - - - -
which was rediculous of Nutkin,
because he hadn't got any ring to
give to old Brown.

The fifth day the squirrels came
again and brought a present of a
comb of wild honey. It was so
sweet that they liched their fingers
when they put
it down upon
the stone.

But Nutkin danced about, as saucy

as ever and sang —
 "Old Mr B! riddle-me-ree?
 As I went over Tipple Tine,
 I met a flock of bonny swine;
  Some green-lapp'd
  Some green-back'd,
They were the very bonniest swine,
That e'er went over Tipple Tine!
Hum-a-bum, bum, buz. 3·3·3·3 ·
  - - - - - - - - -

Old Brown turned up his nose in
disgust at the impertinence of
Nutkin. But he ate up the honey

The sixth day, which was Saturday,
the squirrels came for the last time.
They brought a parting present for
Old Brown, consisting of a pie with
4 & 20 black birds.

But I am sorry to say that
Nutkin was more saucy and excited
than ever.

He jumped up and down and sang
"Old Mr B! riddle me-ree?
Humpty Dumpty lies in the beck
with a white counterpane round his neck,
All the king's horses, and all the king's men,
Can't put Humpty Dumpty
together again!"

Now old Mr Brown took an interest
in eggs; he opened one eye and shut
it again; but still he never said
nothing.   Nutkin got more
and more excited —

　　"Old Mr B. riddle-me-ree?
　Hick-amore, Hach-a-more,
　On the kings kitchen door,
　All the king's horses,
　And all the king's men,
Could n't drive Hick-a-more, Hack-a-more
Off the king's kitchen door!"
　　　- - ʃ- - - — - - ' - -
And nutkin danced up and down
like a sun-beam; but old Mr
Brown never said nothing.
　　Then Nutkin began again —

"Old Mr B! riddle-me-ree?
(Nutkin bounced up & down and
clapped his paws)—
"Old Mr. B! riddle-me-ree?
Arthur O'Bower has broken his band,
He comes roaring up the land;
The king of Scots, with all his power,
Cannot turn Arthur of the Bower!"

Nutkin whisked and twirled and made
a whirring noise like the wind, and
flicked his bushy tail right in the
face of old Brown's whiskers.
Then all at once there was a
flufflement and a scufflement
and a loud "Squeak!!"

The squirrels scuttered away
into the bushes. When they came

back and peeped cautiously round
the tree — there was Old Brown
sitting on his door step, quite still,
with his eyes closed: as if nothing had
happened.

But Nutkin was in his waistcoat
pocket!!!

That is the end of the story. Old
Brown carried Nutkin into his
house, and held him up by the
tail, intending to skin him; but
Nutkin pulled so hard that his tail
broke in two, and he dashed
up the stair-case, and escaped out of
the attic window.

And to this day, if you meet
Nutkin up a tree, and ask him a
riddle, he will throw sticks at you,
and chatter his teeth, and scold,
and shout — "Cuck cuck cuck cuck
Cur-rrr."!

Yours aff. Beatrix Potter

Background for Owl Island

"St. Herbert's Island, Derwentwater" from a Sketch Book

SQUIRREL NUTKIN (1903)

" They made little rafts out of twigs, and they paddled
away over the water to Owl Island to gather nuts "

Duplicate Original

*The term " duplicate original " indicates that this drawing was similar to,
but not the actual one used in the book.

O

Background Sketch

Where " the squirrels filled their little sacks with nuts "

" The squirrels filled their little sacks with nuts, and
sailed away home in the evening "

Original

" The squirrels brought a present of six fat beetles . . . Each beetle
was wrapped up carefully in a dock-leaf, fastened with a pine-
needle-pin "

Original

" Nutkin gathered robin's pin-cushions off a briar bush "

Original

TAILOR OF GLOUCESTER (1903)

Facsimile from the Original Manuscript   *Unfinished*

the tailor was so poor he only rented
the kitchen. He lived there with his
cat; it was called Simpkin.

Now all day long while the tailor
was out at work, Simpkin kept house
all alone; and he also was fond
of the mice, though he gave them
no satin for coats!
"Miaw"? said the cat when the tailor
opened the door, "Miaw?"
The tailor replied— "Simpkin, we shall
make our fortune, but I am worn
to a ravelling. Take this groat
(which is our last fourpence) and
Simpkin, take a china pipkin; buy a
penn'orth of bread, a penn'orth of milk and
a penn'orth of sausages. And O Simpkin,
with the last penny of our fourpence

Facsimile from the Original Manuscript. (Warne's Edition)

" The tailor sat down, close over the fire, lamenting—
. . . The little mice came out again, and listened to the
tailor . . . "

Duplicate Original

A " satin waistcoat—trimmed with gauze and green worsted chenille—for the Mayor of Gloucester "

Original

" There was a snippeting of scissors, and snappeting of thread "   *Original*

" He made the most wonderful waistcoats "   *Original*

THE ART OF BEATRIX POTTER

Six sketches used for background in

BENJAMIN BUNNY

" The proper way to get in, is to climb down a pear tree "   Sept. 8th, 1903

" The lettuces certainly were very fine "   July 28th, 1903

" They went along a little walk on planks "   Summer, 1903

" They went along a little walk on planks, under a sunny
red-brick wall "

Original

" They got amongst flower-pots, and frames and tubs "   Sept. 1903

The corner of the garden where Benjamin and Peter hid under the basket

Background Sketch   Sept. 11th, 1903

The gate through which old Mr. Bunny " marched out of the garden "

Summer, 1903

" He suggested that they should fill the pocket-handkerchief with onions "

Original

*Old Mr. Bunny whips his nephew Peter

*This drawing was used in " Peter Rabbit's Painting Book," 1911, with the title,
" They will not go to Mr. McGregor's garden again."

" Old Mr. Bunny . . . took out his son Benjamin by the ears,
and whipped him with a little switch.   Then he took out
his nephew Peter "

Original

TWO BAD MICE (1904)

" As the fish would not come off the plate, they put it into the red-hot crinkly paper fire in the kitchen "

Original

" She found some tiny canisters upon the dresser, labelled—
Rice—Coffee—Sago—but when she turned them upside
down, there was nothing inside except red and blue beads "

Original

" But the nurse said—" I will set a mouse trap ! "   *Original*

" He found a crooked sixpence . . . he and Hunca Munca stuffed it into one
of the stockings of Lucinda and Jane "

Original

MRS. TIGGY WINKLE (1905)

" And besides—*I* have seen that door into the back of the hill called Cat Bells "

Background Sketch

Rough Sketches of Lucie and the little door in the back of the hill

Mrs. Tiggy-Winkle with an iron in her hand   *Original*

" And she hung up all sorts and sizes of clothes— "   *Original*

THE PIE AND THE PATTY PAN (1905)

Water-colour used as background for " The Invitation "

Note : See Fig. 18, *page* 329.

" The Invitation "   *Original*

Background Sketch used for " The Veal and Ham Pie "

" The Veal and Ham Pie "   *Original*

Note: See Figs. 19 *and* 20, *pages* 330 *and* 331.

"The Pie and the Patty-pan."

Once upon a time there was a Pussy
-cat called Ribby, who invited a
little dog — called Duchess — to tea.
    "Come in good time, my dear Duchess
(said Ribby's letter) "and we will have
something so very very nice. I am
baking it in a pie-dish. — a pie-dish
with a pink rim. You never
tasted anything so good!
And you shall eat it all! I will
eat muffins, my dear Duchess!"
wrote Ribby.
        Duchess read the letter and wrote
an answer — "I will come with
much pleasure at a quarter past 4.
    But it is very strange, I was just
going to write to you, my dear Ribby
to invite you here to supper, to eat

Facsimile from the Original Manuscript

Something most delicious.
I will come very punctually, my
dear Ribby" — wrote Duchess; and
then at the end she wrote —
"I hope it isn't mouse.?"
And then she thought that did not
sound very polite; so she scratched
out "isn't mouse?" and changed it
to "I hope it will be fine," and
she gave her letter to the postman.
But she thought a great deal
about Ribby's pie. "I am dreadfully
afraid it will be mouse!" said
Duchess to herself — "I really
couldn't, couldn't eat mouse-pie.
And I shall have to eat it,
because it is a party. And my
pie was going to be veal and ham.
A pink & white pie dish! and so
is mine; just like Ribby's dishes;

Facsimile from the Original Manuscript

" In Mrs. Lord's cottage. Lakefield Cottage, Sawrey, used for Pie and Patty Pan "

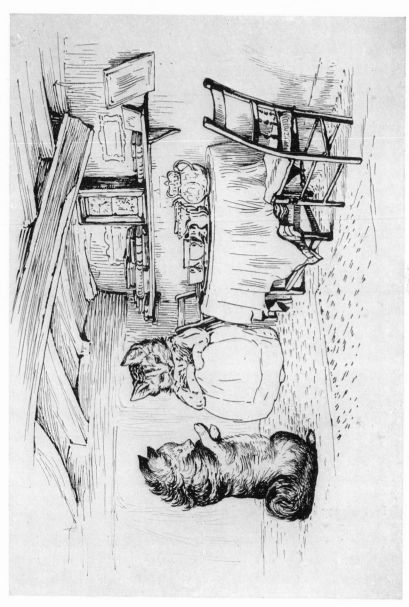

An unpublished drawing of Duchess and Ribby

MR. JEREMY FISHER (1906)

Preliminary Sketch of Mr. Jeremy Fisher

" For nearly an hour he stared at the float "   *Original*

" The boat was round and green, and very like the other lily-leaves "

Original

" Mr. Jeremy bounced up to the surface of the water, like a cork. . . "

Original

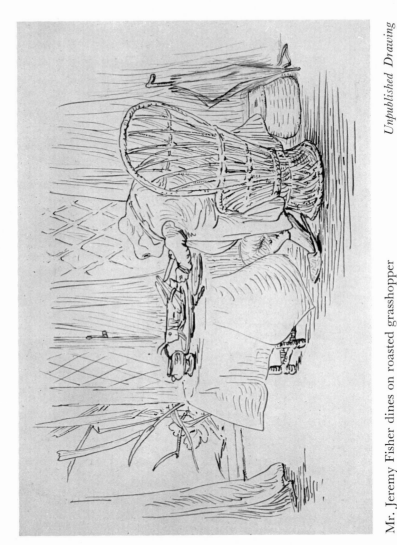

Unpublished Drawing

Mr. Jeremy Fisher dines on roasted grasshopper

" Mrs. Tabitha Twitchit . . . fetched the kittens indoors, to wash and dress them "

Original

Note : See Fig. 2, *page* 313.

" Tabitha Twitchit came down the garden and found her
kittens on the wall with no clothes on "

Original

Mrs. Tabitha Twitchit receives friends to tea   *Original*

JEMIMA PUDDLE-DUCK (1908)

Jemima and the gentleman with sandy whiskers   *Original*

" ' I wish to hatch my own eggs ; I will hatch them all by myself,'
quacked Jemima Puddle-Duck "

Original

Note : See Fig. 9, page 320.

255

" When she reached the top of the hill, she saw a wood in the distance "

Original

Note : See Fig. 12, *page* 323.

" She rather fancied a tree-stump amongst some tall fox-gloves "

Original

THE ROLY-POLY PUDDING (1908)

" ' I'm in sad trouble, Cousin Ribby,' said Tabitha, shedding tears. ' I've lost my dear son Thomas . . .' "

Original

" Mrs. Tabitha Twitchit searching for her son Thomas " *Duplicate Original*

" The visitor was a neighbour, Mrs. Ribby ; she had called to borrow some yeast "

Original

Note : See Fig. 3, *page* 314.

" They had been obliged to put Tom Kitten into a hot bath to get the butter off "

Original

" The chimney stack stood up above the roof like a little stone tower "

Original

Note : See Fig. 13, *page* 324.

" Benjamin used to borrow cabbages from Flopsy's brother, Peter Rabbit, who kept a nursery garden "

Original (1st Edition only)

Water-colour used as background for the Village Shop.   *Ginger and Pickles 1909.*   (Old Mr. John Taylor's shop, Sawrey)

The Village Shop   *Original*

" Mr. John Dormouse and his daughter began to sell peppermints and candles "

Original

" Such a funny house ! There were yards and
yards of sandy passages, leading to storerooms
and nut-cellars and seed-cellars, all amongst the
roots of the hedge "

Original

TIMMY TIPTOES (1911)

" Silvertail digs for nuts " *Original*

" They crept up to the bedroom window "   *Original*

PIGLING BLAND (1913)

Alexander and Pigling Bland at the Cross-roads   *Duplicate Original*

Note: See Fig. 21, *page* 332.

Water-colour used as background for the Kitchen scenes in Pigling Bland.
(" Spout House," Far Sawrey)

You know the old woman
Who lived in a shoe ?
And had so many children
She didn't know what to do ?

Duplicate Original

I think if she lived in
   a little shoe-house—
That little old woman was
   surely a mouse !

Duplicate Original

JOHNNY TOWN-MOUSE (1918)

" The Town Mouse and the Country Mouse "   *Unpublished*

" The Country Mouse and the Town Mouse "   *Unpublished*

Original version of the opening pages of
CECILY PARSLEY

Cecily Parsley lived
in a Pen,
And brewed good ale
for
Gentlemen.

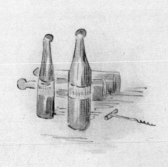

Gentlemen

came every

Day —

Till

Cecily Parsley ran

Away!

January, 1897

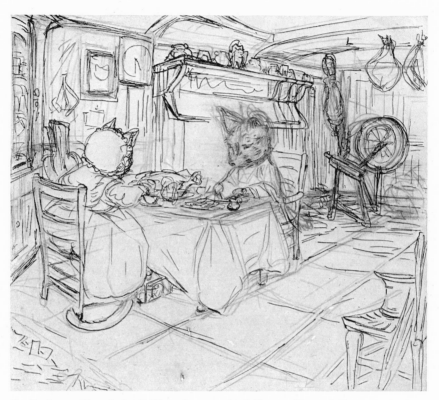

Preliminary Sketch for " How do you do, Mistress Pussy ? "

" How do you do, Mistress Pussy ?
Mistress Pussy, how do you do ? "
" I thank you kindly, little dog,
I fare as well as you ! "

Original

281

Preliminary Sketch for The Guinea-pigs' Garden

Duplicate Original

The Guinea-pigs' Garden

Bow, wow, wow !
  Whose dog art thou ?
" I'm little Tom Tinker's dog,
  Bow, wow, wow ! "

Original

" There were crowds in the street, as it was market day "

Original

THE FAIRY CARAVAN

"Louisa Pussy-cat sleeps late"   *Original*

10

MISCELLANY

MINIATURE LETTERS

These letters were written by Beatrix Potter as from some of the characters in her books. Each letter was shaped and folded to represent an envelope. Some were sent to children of the Moore family and posted in a miniature Mail Bag which she made herself and inscribed with the letters G.P.O. Others were sent to Master Drew Fayle, and to " Lucie " of Newlands and her little sister.

SQUIRREL NUTKIN

MR. BROWN, OWL ISLAND.

Sir, I should esteem it a favour if you would let me have back my tail, as I miss it very much. I would pay postage.
Yrs. truly, Squirrel Nutkin.

MR. OLD BROWN ESQ., OWL ISLAND.

Dear Sir, I should be extremely obliged if you could kindly send back a tail which you have had for some time. It is fluffy brown with a white tip. I wrote to you before about it, but perhaps I did not address the letter properly. I will pay the postage. Yrs. respectifully, Sq. Nutkin.

OLD MR. BROWN ESQ., OWL ISLAND.

Dear Sir, I should be exceedingly obliged if you will let me have back my tail, I will gladly pay 3 bags of nuts for it if you will please post it back to me, I have written to you twice Mr. Brown, I think I did not give my address, it is Derwent Bay Wood, Yrs. respectifully, Sq. Nutkin.

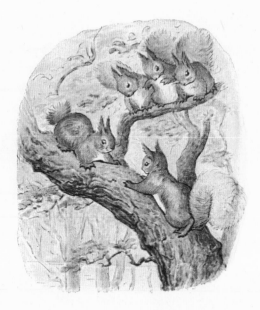

" And to this day, if you meet Nutkin up a tree and
ask him a riddle, he will throw sticks at you . . . "

O. BROWN ESQ., M.P., OWL ISLAND.

Dear Sir, I write on behalf of my brother Nutkin to beg that as a great favour
you would send him back his tail. He never makes—or asks—riddles now, and
he is truly sorry that he was so rude. Trusting that you continue to enjoy good
health, I remain Yr. obedient servant, Twinkleberry Squirrel.

MASTER SQUIRREL NUTKIN, DERWENT BAY WOOD.

Mr. Brown writes to say that he cannot reply to letters as he is asleep. Mr.
Brown cannot return the tail. He ate it some time ago ; it nearly choked
him. Mr. Brown requests Nutkin not to write again, as his repeated letters
are a nuisance.

T

TWO BAD MICE

Hunca Munca comes with her dust-
pan and her broom to sweep the Doll's
house !

MRS. THOMAS THUMB, MOUSE HOLE.

Miss Lucinda Doll will require Hunca Munca to come for the whole day
on Saturday. Jane Dollcook has had an accident. She has broken the soup
tureen and both her wooden legs.

MISS LUCINDA DOLL, DOLL'S HOUSE.

Honoured Madam, I thank you kindly for your letter informing me that
Tom Kitten is coming to sweep the kitchen chimney at 6. I will arrive
punctually at 7. Thanking you for past favours. Yr. obedient servant, Hunca
Munca.

MISCELLANY

Miss Lucinda Doll, Doll's House.

Honoured Madam, Would you forgive my asking whether you can spare a feather bed ? The feathers are all coming out of the one we stole from your house. If you can spare another, me & my wife would be truly grateful. Yr. obedient humble servant, Thomas Thumb.
P.S. Me & my wife are grateful to you for employing her as char-woman. I hope that she continues to give satisfaction.

Mr. T. Thumb, Mouse Hole.

Miss Lucinda Doll has received Tom Thumb's appeal, but she regrets to inform Tom Thumb that she has never had another feather bed for *herself*. She also regrets to say that Hunca Munca forgot to dust the mantelpiece on Wednesday.

Miss Lucinda Doll, Doll's House.

Honoured Madam, I am sorry to hear that my wife forgot to dust the mantelpiece, I have whipped her. Me & my wife would be very grateful for another kettle, the last one is full of holes. Me & my wife do not think that it was made of tin at all. We have nine of a family at present & they require hot water. I remain honoured madam. Yr. obedient servant, Thomas Thumb.

Honoured Madam
I am sorry to hear that my wife forgot to dust the mantelpiece, I have whipped her. Me & my wife would be very grateful for another kettle, the last one is full of holes. Me & my wife do not think that it was made of tin at all..
we have nine of a family at present & they require hot water
I remain honoured madam yr obedient servant
Thomas Thumb

MRS. TIGGY WINKLE

MRS. RABBIT, SAND BANK, UNDER FIR-TREE.

If you please'm, Indeed I appologize sincerely for the starchiness & hope you will forgive me if you please mum, indeed it is Tom Titmouse and the rest of them ; they do want their collar that starchy if you please mum my mind do get mixed up. If you please I will wash the clothes without charge for a fortnight if you will give another trial to your obedient servant & washerwoman Tiggy Winkle.

MASTER D. FAYLE, KYLIMORE, CO. DUBLIN.

Dear Drew, I have got that mixed up with this week's wash ! Have *you* got Mrs. Flopsy Bunny's shirt or Mr. Jeremy Fisher's apron ? instead of your pocket handkerchief—I mean to say Mrs. Flopsy Bunny's apron. Everything is all got mixed up in wrong bundles. I will buy more safety pins. Yr. aff. washerwoman T. Winkle.

MASTER D. FAYLE, KYLIMORE.

Dear Drew, I hope that your washing is done to please you ? I consider that Mrs. Tiggy Winkle is particularly good at ironing collars ; but she does mix things up at the wash. I have got a shirt marked J.F. instead of an apron. Have you lost a shirt at the wash ? It is 3 inches long. My apron is much larger and marked F.B. Yrs. Flopsy Bunny.

" Oh, that's a pair of stockings belonging
to Sally Henny-penny."

MRS. TIGGY WINKLE, CAT BELLS.

Mr. J. Fisher regrets that he has to complain about the washing. Mrs. T. W.
has sent home an immense white apron with tapes instead of Mr. J. F's best
new shirt. The apron is marked " F. B. "

Jan. 22, 1910

MRS. TIGGY WINKLE, CAT BELLS.

Mr. J. Fisher regrets to have to complain again about the washing. Mrs.
T. Winkle has sent home an enormous handkerchief marked " D. Fayle "
instead of the tablecloth marked J. F.

If this continues every week, Mr. J. Fisher will have to get married, so as to
have the washing done at home.

THE ART OF BEATRIX POTTER

MR. JEREMY FISHER

MASTER D. FAYLE, KYLIMORE.

Dear Master Drew, I hear that you think that there ought to be a " Mrs. J. Fisher ". Our friend is at present taking mud baths at the bottom of the pond, which may be the reason why your letter has not been answered quick by return. I will do my best to advise him, but I fear he remembers the sad fate of his elder brother who disobeyed his mother, and he was gobbled up by a lily white duck ! If my friend Jeremy gets married, I will certainly tell you, & send a bit of wedding cake. One of our friends is going into the next book. He is fatter than Jeremy ; and he has shorter legs. Yrs. with compliments, Sir Isaac Newton.

MASTER DREW FAYLE, KYLIMORE.

Dear Master Drew, I hear that you are interested in the domestic arrangements of our friend Jeremy Fisher. I am of opinion that his dinner parties would be much more agreeable if there were a lady to preside at the table. I do not care for roast grasshoppers. His housekeeping and cookery do not come up to the standard to which I am accustomed at the Mansion House. Yrs. truly, Alderman Pt. Tortoise.

MASTER D. FAYLE, KYLIMORE, CO. DUBLIN.

Dear Master Drew, In answer to your very kind inquiry, I live alone ; I am not married. When I bought my sprigged waistcoat & my maroon tail-coat I had hopes . . . . But I am alone . . . If there were a " Mrs. Jeremy Fisher " she might object to snails. It is some satisfaction to be able to have as much water & mud in the house as a person likes. Thanking you for your touching inquiry. Yr. devoted friend Jeremiah Fisher.

294

" The water was all slippy-sloppy in the larder
and in the back passage "

MASTER DREW FAYLE, KYLIMORE, CO. DUBLIN.

Dear Master Drew, If you please Sir I am a widow ; & I think it is very wrong
that there is not any Mrs. Jeremy Fisher, but *I* would not marry Mr. Jeremy
not for worlds, the way he does live in that house all slippy-sloppy ; not any
lady would stand it, & not a bit of good starching his cravats. Yr. obedient
washerwoman, Tiggy Winkle.

Mr. Alderman Ptolemy Tortoise Request the pleasure of Sir Isaac Newton's Company at Dinner on Dec. 25th (to meet our friend Fisher) R.S.V.P.

MR. ALDERMAN PTOLEMY TORTOISE, THE MELON PIT.

Dear Mr. Alderman, I shall have much pleasure in dining with you on Dec. 25th. It is a surprise as I thought that you were asleep. Perhaps the present disagreeable frost has not yet penetrated into the general atmosphere of the Melon Pit. Our friend Fisher was taking mud baths at the bottom of the pond when last I heard of him.

Faithfully yrs.

I. Newton.

" They had a roasted grasshopper with lady-bird sauce "

The miniature Mail Bag made by Beatrix Potter for use with the letters.

For some other children Beatrix Potter placed these miniature letters in a toy post box of bright red tin, resembling the post boxes placed on country walls.   The box containing the letters was then sent to the children.

THE PIE AND THE PATTY PAN

Mrs. Duchess, Belle Green.

My Dear Duchess, If you are at home and not engaged will you come to tea tomorrow ? but if you are away I shall put this in the post and invite cousin Tabitha Twitchit. There will be a red herring, & muffins & crumpets. The patty pans are all locked up. Do come. Yr. aff. friend Ribby—

Mrs. Tabitha Twitchit, Hill Top Farm.

Dear Cousin Tabitha, If you can leave your family with safety I shall be much pleased if you will take tea with me this afternoon. There will be muffins and crumpets and a red herring. I have just been to call upon my friend Duchess, she is away from home. Yr. aff. cousin, Ribby.

The Invitation

MISCELLANY

Mrs. Ribstone Pippin, Lakefield Cottage.

Dear Cousin Ribby, I shall be pleased to take tea with you. I am glad that Duchess is away from home, I do not care for dogs. My son Thomas is well, but he grows out of all his clothes, and I have other troubles. Yr. aff. cousin Tabitha Twitchit.

Mrs. Ribstone Pippin, Lakefield Cottage.

My dear Ribby, I am so sorry I was out, it would have given me so much pleasure to accept your kind invitation. I had gone to a dog show. I enjoyed it very much but I am a little disappointed that I did not take a prize and I missed the red herring. Yr. aff. friend, Duchess.

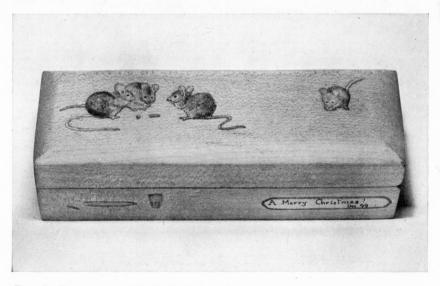

Beatrix Potter gave this little box to her mother, Christmas, 1899. The figures of mice are painted in water colour, cut out, and pasted on the box
(Full size)

Designs from a Set of Dinner Cards

The original version of Chapter VI of

" THE FAIRY CARAVAN "

Once upon a time there was a little
mouse and she was asked to a
wedding. Said she to herself—
"What shall I wear? what shall I
wear? There is a tear in my old
gray gown, and the shops are shut
on a Wednesday!"
And while she was turning over
her clothes, there came a knock
at the house door and when she opened
it, there was an green pedler
caterpiller-man, who said —
"Any-lace-tape- twine-silk-caterpillar
twist or fine netted Today
Mam?" And the mouse bought
some caterpiller twine 7 pins 2 peppercorns
but she wouldn't like his spotted silk
7 she shut the door on him 7 he
went away very sulky 7 let himself

down by a thread from the attic
window to shew how strong it
was.

And next came another tap at
the door & when she opened it
there was a little old spider pedlar
woman who made a bob curtsey and
said "any lace turn twist or
fine gossamer spider web, that the
black & white spiders have spun in
a holly bush?" And the little
mouse paid her 5 pepper corns &
bought bobbins & bobbins of it!
And because it was so very very
fine she got out her spinning
wheel & twisted 3 threads together
into a stronger thread.

And when she had spun enough
twist she took it in a basket & ran

along the rafters, up into the roof
where the great brown house spiders
live, ? she went to a spider that
was a weaver ? had a loom,
? he wove a ~~fine~~ piece of ~~spider~~ cobweb
~~web~~ silk,, ? the treadles went
that glistered like green gold
clickitty bump, clickitty bump ?
the shuttle jigged to ? fro, ?
the little mouse paid him 6
pepper corns for his weaving.
And the humble bee lent her some
wax to her thread, and the crickets
that nibble the woolens did lend
her their scissors; and the little
mouse danced at the wedding!

" They trod a circle on the snow around the Christmas Tree "

(*Design for a Christmas Card for the Invalid Children's Aid Association*)

Between the stream and the tree where the hens were roosting, there was a white untrodden slope.   Only one tree grew there, a very small spruce, a little Christmas tree some four foot high. As the night grew darker — the branches of this little tree became all tipped with light, and wreathed with icicles and chains of frost.   Brighter and brighter it shone, until it seemed to bear a hundred fairy lights.

Not like the yellow gleam of candles; but a clear white incandescent light.   Small voices and music began to mingle with the sound of the water.   Up by the snowy banks, from the wood and from the meadow beyond, tripped scores of little shadowy creatures, advancing from the darkness into the light.   They trod a circle on the snow around the Christmas tree, dancing gaily hand-in-hand.   Rabbits, voles, squirrels and wood-mice — even the half blind mole, old Samson velvet, danced hand-in-paw with a wood mouse and a shrew — whilst a hedgehog played the bag-pipes beneath the fairy spruce.

From " The Fairy Caravan " pages 127-128
Facsimile from the Original Manuscript

This is a feather of poor old
— "Charles" —
Who died lamented and respected
on Nov 17th. 1929.
He was 8½ years old, and had
never been beaten in battle.
The hens are quite well
thank you!

Beatrix Potter
Nov 22. 29.

" The homestead of Codlin Croft was dominated by Charles, our cock . . . "

" The Fairy Caravan " page 112
(*Published privately, October,* 1929)

Henny Penny, mother of Charles, was a wonderful layer, and she laid immense white eggs. I could always pick out her eggs in the basket — but the difficulty first was to find them!

I think Jemima Puddleduck might have taken a lesson from her in the art of hiding nests.

" Sally Henny Penny sent out a printed poster to say that she was going to re-open the shop—"

" *Ginger and Pickles* "

And so soon as we had tracked her, and found her nest — in the barn — she returned to the hay rack in the stable — or the coal house — or the pig stye — or the ash pit — Fortunately she chose a ledge high up under the pig stye roof, which no pig could reach. I have a pleasing recollection of Henny Penny's large white shiny eggs — one of which hatched into that remarkable bird Charles.

Beatrix Potter
Nov 21st 29

Design for a Christmas Card for the Invalid Children's
Aid Association

A " Peter Rabbit " design for a Christmas Card

PHOTOGRAPHS OF HILL TOP AND SAWREY ASSOCIATED WITH BEATRIX POTTER AND HER BOOKS

Beatrix Potter at Hill Top   (About 1907)

Fig. 1. Hill Top, Sawrey, in the late Spring

Fig. 2. The path leading to Hill Top

Fig. 3. Interior—Hill Top

Fig. 4. Interior—Hill Top

Fig. 5.   Interior—Hill Top

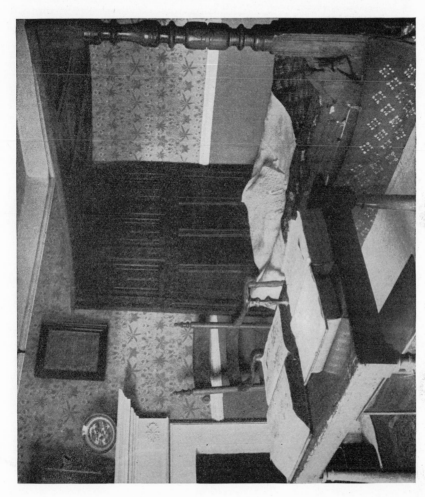

Fig. 6. Interior—Hill Top

Fig. 7.   The Gate, looking from the porch of Hill Top

Fig. 8.   Sheep at Hill Top Farm

Fig. 9.   The Farmyard at Hill Top

Fig. 10.   The Cart Road leading over the hill, at Hill Top Farm

W

Fig. 11.   The view from Hill Top Farm looking towards the wood

Fig. 12.   The view from Hill Top Farm looking beyond Esthwaite Water to the Coniston Fells

Fig. 13. The Village of Sawrey as seen from Hill Top Farm

Fig. 14.   Castle Cottage, Sawrey

(*The low hedge in the foreground has been planted since the death of Mrs. Heelis.*)

Fig. 15.   The end of Smithy Lane—approach to Castle Cottage

Fig. 16. The village street—otherwise "Smithy Lane"

Fig. 17. Sawrey Village

Fig. 18.   A Garden in Sawrey

Fig. 19.   The Sawrey Post Office of earlier times

Fig. 20. The Sawrey Post Office of earlier times

Fig. 21.   The Cross-roads

(On the left the road leads to Lakeside, and on the right to Hawkshead.)

APPENDIX

333

THE BEATRIX POTTER BOOKS

(Published by F. Warne & Co. Ltd., unless otherwise stated)

1	The Tale of Peter Rabbit (privately printed)	1901
	(The first privately printed (flat-back) edition, 250 copies, Dec. 1901, was followed by a second privately printed (round-back) edition, 200 copies, Feb. 1902).	
2	The Tale of Peter Rabbit	1902
3	The Tailor of Gloucester (privately printed)	1902
	(500 copies, Dec. 1902).	
4	The Tale of Squirrel Nutkin	1903
5	The Tailor of Gloucester	1903
6	The Tale of Benjamin Bunny	1904
7	The Tale of Two Bad Mice	1904
8	The Tale of Mrs. Tiggy-Winkle	1905
9	*The Pie and the Patty-pan	1905
10	The Tale of Mr. Jeremy Fisher	1906
11	The Story of a Fierce Bad Rabbit (Panoramic Form)	1906
12	The Story of Miss Moppet (Panoramic Form)	1906
13	The Tale of Tom Kitten	1907
14	The Tale of Jemima Puddle-Duck	1908
15	*The Roly-Poly Pudding	1908
16	The Tale of the Flopsy Bunnies	1909
17	*Ginger and Pickles	1909
18	The Tale of Mrs. Tittlemouse	1910
19	Peter Rabbit's Painting Book	1911
20	The Tale of Timmy Tiptoes	1911

*First published in the larger size format.

APPENDIX

TRANSLATIONS INTO OTHER LANGUAGES
(Identical in form with the English editions)

*First published in the larger size format.
†First English edition, July, 1952.

THE ART OF BEATRIX POTTER

Dutch	Het Verhaal van Pieter Langoor (Peter Rabbit)	1912
	Benjamin Knabbel (Benjamin Bunny)	1946
	Twee Stoute Muisjes (Two Bad Mice)	1946
	Jeremias de Hengelaar (Mr. Jeremy Fisher)	1946
	Tom Het Poesje (Tom Kitten)	1946
	Het Verhaal van Kwakkel Waggel-Eend (Jemima Puddle-Duck)	1912
	De Kleine Langoortjes (Flopsy Bunnies)	1946
Welsh	Hanes Pwtan y Wningen (Peter Rabbit)	1932
	Hanes Benda Bynni (Benjamin Bunny)	1948
	Hanes Meistres Tigi-Dwt (Mrs. Tiggy-Winkle)	1932
	Hanes Dili Minllyn (Jemima Puddle-Duck)	1924
German	Die Geschichte des Peterchen Hase (Peter Rabbit)	1934
	Die Geschichte von den zwei bösen Mäuschen (Two Bad Mice)	1939
	Die Geschichte von Frau Tiggy-Winkle (Mrs. Tiggy-Winkle)	1948
	Die Geschichte von Samuel Hagezahn (Samuel Whiskers, or The Roly-Poly Pudding)	1951
	Die Geschichte Der Hasenfamilie Plumps (Flopsy Bunnies)	1947
	Die Geschichte von Herrn Reineke (Mr. Tod)	1951
Italian	Il Coniglio Pierino (Peter Rabbit)	1948
Spanish	Pedrin El Conejo Travieso (Peter Rabbit)	1931
Swedish	Sagan om Pelle Kanin (Peter Rabbit)	1948
	Sagan om Kurre Nötpigg (Squirrel Nutkin)	1954
	Den lillae grisen Robinsons äventyr (no illustrations)	1938
Norwegian	Fortellingen om Nina Pytt-And (Jemima Puddle-Duck)	1948
Danish	Tom Kitte (Tom Kitten)	1946
Afrikaans	Die Verhaal van Pieter Konyntjie (Peter Rabbit)	1929
	Die Verhaal van Bennie Blinkhaar (Benjamin Bunny)	1935
	Die Verhaal van Die Flopsie-Familie (Flopsy Bunnies)	1935
	Die Verhaal van Mevrou Piekfyn (Mrs. Tittlemouse)	1935